Hibernation

Anita Ganeri

Heinemann Library
Chicago, Illinois

2005 Heinemann Library
a division of Reed Elsevier Inc.
Chicago, Illinois

Customer Service 888-454-2279

Visit our website at www.heinemannlibrary.com

Designed by Jo Malivoire
Printed and bound in China by South China Printing Company

09 08 07 06 05
10 9 8 7 6 5 4 3 2 1

Library of Congress Cataloging-in-Publication Data
Ganeri, Anita, 1961-
  Hibernation / Anita Ganeri.
      p. cm. — (Nature's patterns)
  Includes bibliographical references and index.
  ISBN 1-4034-5895-2 (hc) — ISBN 1-4109-1318-X (pbk.)
  1. Hibernation—Juvenile literature. I. Title. II. Series.
  QL755.G36 2004
  591.56'5—dc22
                              2004007464

Acknowledgments
The author and publishers are grateful to the following for permission to reproduce copyright
material: p. **4** George McCarthy/Nature Photo Library; p. **5** David Tipling/Nature Photo Library;
p. **6** Peter Johnson/Corbis; pp. **7, 8, 12, 15, 16, 20, 23, 29** OSF; p. **9** Kennan Ward/Corbis;
pp. **10, 14** Corbis; p. **11** Rich Kirchner/NHPA; p. **13** Daniel Heuclin/NHPA; p. **17** Paul
Hobson/Nature Photo Library; p. **18** Eric Soder/NHPA; p. **19** Ingo Arndt/Nature Photo Library;
p. **21** Anthony Bannister/NHPA; p. **22** Robert Thompson/NHPA; p. **24** George D Lepp/Corbis; p.
25 Asgeir Helgestad/Nature Photo Library; p. **26** Steven David Miller/Nature Photo Library
p. **27** Alfo/Nature Photo Library; p. **28** V Hurst and T Kitchin/NHPA.

Cover photograph of a hibernating dormouse by Nature Photo Library.

Every effort has been made to contact copyright holders of any material reproduced in this book.
Any omissions will be rectified in subsequent printings if notice is given to the publisher.

Some words are shown in bold, **like this**. You can find out what
they mean by looking in the glossary.

Contents

Nature's Patterns

Nature is always changing. Many of the changes that happen follow a **pattern.** This means that they happen over and over again.

This sleeping dormouse will wake up in spring.

The poorwill from North America is the only bird that hibernates.

Hibernation is like a very deep sleep. It is a pattern that usually happens each year. Many animals hibernate at the beginning of winter. Then they wake up again in spring.

Winter Sleep

Winter is a hard time for animals. The weather can be very cold, and there is not much food to eat. Some animals have to **hibernate** to stay alive.

These ground squirrels sleep right through winter.

Sometimes bears wake up to eat during their long sleep.

Some animals sleep very deeply when they hibernate. They hardly breathe and their heart beats very slowly. Other animals doze off, but they wake up from time to time.

7

Storing fat

An Alpine marmot eats lots of seeds before it hibernates.

In summer animals get ready to **hibernate.** Some animals eat a lot of extra food and get very fat. In winter they use their stored fat to stay alive.

A brown bear gathers berries to get ready for winter.

Animals such as bears collect
lots of fruit, nuts, and berries.
They hide this food in their
burrows or **dens.** They snack
on it during the winter.

A Place to Sleep

Animals must find a safe place to sleep. Some animals dig **dens** and **burrows.** Others look for caves and hollow trees. Some animals **hibernate** under stones or piles of leaves.

Polar bears dig their dens in the snow.

In fall animals get their sleeping places ready. Some animals collect grass and leaves to put in their burrows. This helps keep them warm in winter.

Marmots line their burrows with soft grass.

Settling Down

Some animals **hibernate** alone. They hide away in a hole or **den** and quickly fall asleep. A toadfish digs a **burrow** in the mud on the bottom of the sea.

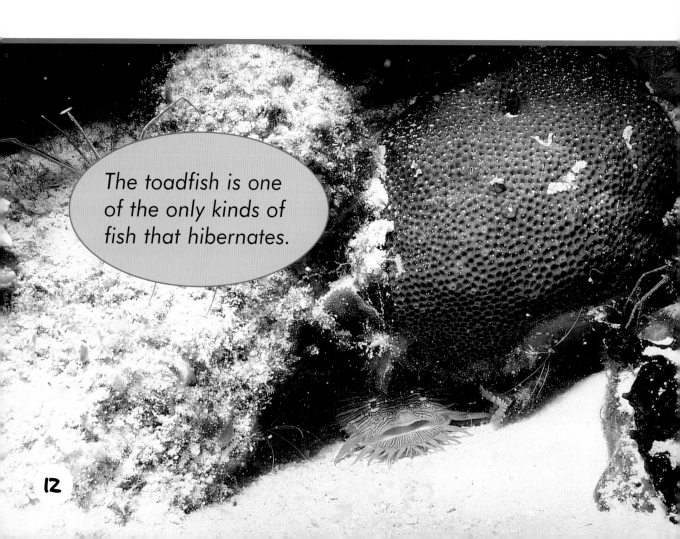

The toadfish is one of the only kinds of fish that hibernates.

Animals such as bats, snakes, and butterflies hibernate in big groups. This is so they can huddle together and stay warm.

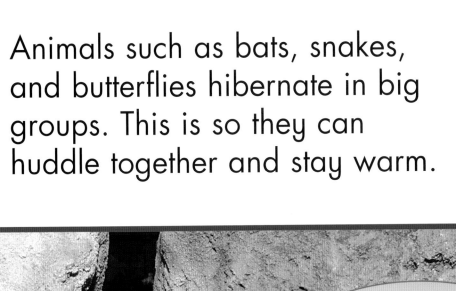

Rattlesnakes sometimes hibernate in groups.

Slowing Down

When an animal **hibernates,** it falls into a deep sleep. Its body works more slowly than usual. Its heart beats very slowly, and its breathing slows down.

A woodchuck's body works very slowly while it is asleep.

An animal's body gets colder because its **temperature** drops. All of these changes help the animal save **energy** until it wakes up in spring.

A hibernating bat can get so cold that ice sticks to its body.

15

Food and Waste

Some animals sleep right through the winter. They do not eat anything. Other animals do not sleep so deeply.

Chipmunks wake up to eat food they have stored in their **burrows.**

Some animals, such as hedgehogs, wake up every few weeks. They eat or drink something, and they pass wastes. Then they go back to sleep.

Hedgehogs leave their **dens** to eat.

Sleepyheads

Some **hibernating** animals go to sleep almost as soon as the cold weather begins. Others go through a sleepy time before they finally fall asleep.

Fire salamanders become sleepy during the winter.

Alpine marmots sleep for months when they hibernate.

Some animals stay asleep for a few months. Others sleep for only a few weeks. Alpine marmots are real sleepyheads. They can sleep for more than six months.

19

Waking Up

When spring comes, the **hibernating** animals start to wake up. They know that it is time to wake up because the weather gets warmer.

A groundhog leaves its **burrow** in the spring.

A toad comes out of its winter burrow in the mud.

The animals have to wake up very slowly or they might die. Their bodies begin to warm up and they start to move around.

A Good Meal

Many **hibernating** animals do not eat very much. They live off fat in their bodies or food they have stored. They lose a lot of weight while they are asleep.

When butterflies wake up in spring, they need to find flowers to feed on.

In spring there are berries and fruit to eat.

When animals wake up in the spring, they are thin and hungry. But there is a lot of food around, and they can have a good meal.

Having Babies

In spring the weather is warm, and there is a lot of food to eat. This makes it a good time for many animals to have their babies.

Some animals start to build their nests as soon as they wake up.

In spring and summer, there is lots of food to help bear cubs grow.

Some animals, such as bears, have their babies in their winter **dens.** They **nurse** them through the winter. In spring the mother leaves the den with her **cubs**.

25

Back to Sleep

In fall the weather gets cooler, and it gets darker earlier in the evening. When this happens, animals know that it is time to get ready to **hibernate** again.

A terrapin goes into its **burrow** and gets ready to hibernate.

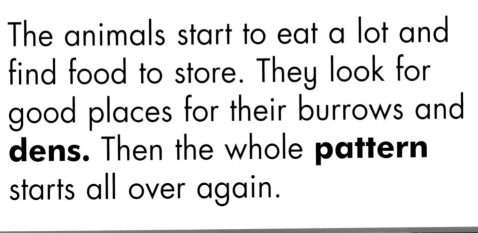

The animals start to eat a lot and find food to store. They look for good places for their burrows and **dens.** Then the whole **pattern** starts all over again.

A golden hamster finds a cosy bed among the leaves.

Cooling Down

In hot places, some animals hide away and sleep when the weather gets very warm and dry. This is a bit like **hibernation,** but it is not the same thing.

Desert toads sleep during very warm, dry weather.

A desert frog sleeps in an underground **burrow** where it is much cooler.

The animals wake up when it starts to rain or when the weather gets cooler. When the weather turns hot and dry, the **pattern** starts all over again.

29

fact file

- Arctic ground squirrels in North America hold the world record for **hibernating.** They sleep for eight months a year.

- Some hibernating bats only breathe once every two hours.

- Terrapins hibernate in the mud at the bottom of a pond. They stay alive by breathing air trapped inside their shells.

Glossary

burrow hole that an animal makes in the ground

cub young bear

den cave or other place where animals can live

energy strength that comes from eating food

hibernate to go into a deep sleep during the winter

nurse to feed and care for a baby animal

pattern something that happens over and over again

temperature how hot or cold something is

More Books to Read

Penny, Malcolm. *Amazing Nature: Hidden Hibernators*. Chicago: Heinemann Library, 2004.

Scrace, Carolyn. *Hibernation (Circle of Life)*. Danbury, Conn: Franklin Watts, 2002.

Wallace, Karen. A Bed for Winter. New York: Dorling Kindersley, 2000.

Index